HICKMANS

North Carolina

Teresa L. Hyman

KIDHAVEN
PRESS™

THOMSON
━━━━━✦━━━━━ ™
GALE

San Diego • Detroit • New York • San Francisco • Cleveland
New Haven, Conn. • Waterville, Maine • London • Munich

© 2003 by KidHaven Press. KidHaven Press is an imprint of The Gale Group, Inc., a division of Thomson Learning, Inc.

KidHaven™ and Thomson Learning™ are trademarks used herein under license.

For more information, contact
KidHaven Press
27500 Drake Rd.
Farmington Hills, MI 48331-3535
Or you can visit our Internet site at http://www.gale.com

LIBRARY OF CONGRESS CATALOGING-IN-PUBLICATION DATA

Hyman, Teresa L.
    North Carolina / by Teresa L. Hyman.
        p.cm.—(Seeds of a nation)
    Summary: Discusses the history of North Carolina, from the lives of the Native Americans who lived there before the European settlers came, through the colonial period, up to its ratification of the United States Constitution in 1789. Includes bibliographical references and index.
    ISBN 0-7377-1420-4 (lib. bdg.: alk. paper)
    1. North Carolina—History—Colonial period, ca. 1600–1775—Juvenile literature. 2. North Carolina—History—1775–1865—Juvenile literature. [1. North Carolina—History Colonial period, ca. 1600-1775.] I. Title. II. Series.
    F257 .H96 2003
    975.6'02—dc21
                                                            2002013975

Printed in the United States of America

Contents

Chapter One

The First North Carolinians

N orth Carolina is rich in history and natural resources. One of the original thirteen colonies, North Carolina is bordered by the Atlantic Ocean to the east, South Carolina and Georgia to the south, Tennessee to the west, and Virginia to the north. From its snow-capped Appalachian Mountains to its beautiful beaches and offshore islands, North Carolina has one of the most diverse climates of any of the fifty states and is the tenth largest state in population, with over 8 million people living there in 2000.

Today, many different groups of people from all around the world live in North Carolina, but the state's original inhabitants were Native Americans. Almost twelve thousand years ago, North Carolina's Native

Americans hunted large beasts such as giant bison and mammoths, fished, and gathered wild fruits and vegetables. As the years passed and the large beasts died out, these Native Americans began growing crops such as corn, beans, and squash, and added those cultivated plants to their diet of wild fruits and animals such as bear, deer, turkey, rabbit, and squirrel. By the time English explorers found the North Carolina coast, twenty to thirty different Native American tribes lived throughout the state.

Though meat was part of their diet, Native Americans of the Carolinas ate mostly fruits, vegetables, and nuts.

Coastal Tribes

Native American tribes speaking different **dialects** of a language called Algonquian lived on the east coast of North America from what is now southern Canada down to the North Carolina–South Carolina border. The largest of the Algonquian-speaking tribes living in North Carolina were the Chowanoc, Pamlico, Croatoan, and Roanoac. These tribes lived in coastal North Carolina from the Outer Banks to the Neuse River. They made round houses, called wigwams, out of woven bark, and lived in villages of up to thirty wigwams. Each village had one chief and each chief used a symbol that conveyed tribal identity. Villagers wore these symbols as tattoos or on their clothing to show where they lived and who their chiefs were.

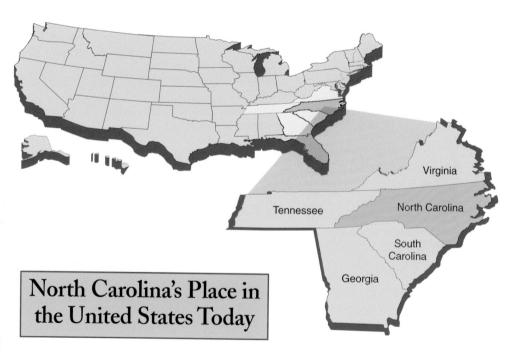

Virginia

Tennessee

North Carolina

South Carolina

Georgia

North Carolina's Place in the United States Today

Native American fishermen of North Carolina use spears and nets to catch fish.

Because they lived in the **tidewater** region of the state, the lifestyle of North Carolina's coastal tribes focused on the water. The men of these tribes made sturdy dugout canoes to navigate and fish the shallow waters of the Atlantic and nearby rivers and streams. They made hooks, spears, and traps to catch fish, lobsters, crabs, and other shellfish that were main parts of their tribal diets. The catch from the nets would be taken back to the village, cooked in pots made from crushed shells or smoked over grills made from reeds or sticks, then stored to be eaten later.

These early coastal North Carolinians also hunted and farmed. Men hunted such animals as deer, bear, turkey, duck, turtle, and alligator while women were in charge of planting such crops as melons, pumpkins, squash, beans, sunflowers, and tobacco, which was not eaten, but used in ceremonies and rituals. In addition to tending the fields, women also made cooking utensils and clothing, took care of the children, and gathered wild fruits and plants for food and medicine.

North Carolina's coastal tribes often traded goods with tribes who lived farther inland. They exchanged beautiful clay tobacco pipes, shells, and beads for the copper, stones, and other items the inland tribes had to offer.

Tribes of the Piedmont and Mountains

Iroquoian-speaking tribes lived in eastern and central North Carolina in a region called the **piedmont**. These tribes migrated from near Lake Ontario and Lake Erie in Canada, down through what are now the states of New York, Pennsylvania, Ohio, Virginia, and Tennessee, to settle in North Carolina. Although the Tuscarora was the largest Iroquoian-speaking tribe living in North Carolina, smaller tribes including the Catechna,

Corn farms like the one pictured here provided crops upon which piedmont tribes depended.

Coree, Neusioc, and Meherrin also lived there. The Cherokee, who lived in the mountains of North Carolina, were also an Iroquoian-speaking tribe.

The tribes of the piedmont were hunters and farmers who lived in long, narrow houses called longhouses. These longhouses were from fifty to three hundred feet

Native Americans dance to thank the Great Spirit for the bounty of their harvest.

long and eighteen to twenty-five feet wide with arched roofs covered with woven bark or grass. Several related families lived in a single longhouse, and several long-houses built close to one another would make up a village. But, unlike the coastal tribes, villages of the piedmont and mountain tribes did not have chiefs. In these tribes, families belonged to different clans. Each clan chose people to represent them at the village council and the council made decisions for the village. When several villages needed to work together, each village council would choose people to represent their village at a tribal council. The tribal council would then make decisions for the group.

Gathering Food

Because the Iroquoian-speaking tribes lived in the fertile piedmont region and in the mountains of North Carolina, they relied more heavily on cultivated crops for food than did the coastal tribes. While the men of these tribes fished and hunted wild game such as bear, deer, and turkey, the women tended to the fields they planted just outside the longhouses. Using hoes made from deer shoulder blades or antlers, women tilled the soil and planted sunflowers, tobacco, pumpkins, and most importantly, squash, corn, and beans. These plants were such staples in their diets that they were called "The Three Sisters." The Cherokee even held a special ceremony each year called the Green Corn Ceremony to thank the Great Spirit for the year's first corn harvest. At the end of the growing season, families would store dried corn and beans in their longhouses in large chests made of tree bark. Dried squash was kept in underground storage places lined with bark and covered with earth. The families within the longhouse would share these food stores throughout the winter.

Border Tribes

The Cherokee tribe in the mountains was separated from their eastern, Iroquoian-speaking relatives by several smaller tribes including the Saponi, Occaneechi, Catawba, and Tutelo. These Siouan-speaking tribes migrated from what is now the midwestern United States—Kansas, Missouri, the Dakotas—and the Lake Michigan and Ohio River areas to settle near the North Carolina–South Carolina border. The largest of North Carolina's Siouan tribes was the Catawba.

Siouan-speaking tribes surrounded their villages and fields with tall wooden fences called palisades to keep out wild animals and provide protection from enemies. Much like their Iroquoian-speaking neighbors, village or tribal councils made most of the decisions for the Siouan tribes, but these tribes also had chiefs to help the councils make decisions. Not much is known about the daily life of these tribes, as they were almost wiped out upon the arrival of European settlers. What is known is that the men of these tribes were skilled hunters who also helped the women clear and till farmland. These women were responsible for growing tobacco, corn, squash, and beans, and children often helped them by pulling up weeds and scaring away

Native American Tribes of North Carolina

▲WEAROEMEOC
▲TUTELO   ▲CHOWANOC
  ▲MEHERRIN
    ▲TUSCARORA
                    ▲PAMLICO
▲CHEROKEE   Raleigh
   Charlotte ▲WAXHAW   ▲ NOTTOWAY
   •
      ▲CATAWBA   ▲ HATTERAS
                              Raleigh
                              Bay

                    Onslow   Pamlico
                    Bay   Sound

▲ Native American Tribes
☐ Present-Day State of
   North Carolina
• Present-Day Cities

                    Atlantic
                    Ocean

birds and small rodents. Siouan children also helped the women gather wild fruits and plants such as the holly plant called the yaupon that was used to make tea.

North Carolina's Native American tribes were friendly toward the state's first explorers and settlers. If it had not been for the coastal tribes and the tribes of the piedmont, the first settlers would not have survived. Those tribes shared their knowledge of North Carolina's rivers and streams, their hunting techniques, and their land with the settlers. Despite their friendliness, however, Native Americans in North Carolina were treated harshly by Europeans. Their tribal lands were taken, often by force, and many were killed or sold into slavery. Exposure to deadly European diseases also greatly decreased their numbers. By 1750 North Carolina's coastal tribes had all but disappeared, and many of the Siouan-speaking tribes had moved or joined with other tribes for survival. By the time North Carolina became a state in 1789, the Cherokee were the only Native Americans of any great number living in the state.

Chapter Two

Early Explorers

In 1524 Giovanni da Verrazano, an Italian captain working for France, sailed his ship, the *Dauphine*, westward from France. Like Christopher Columbus before him, Verrazano was searching for a shortcut from Europe to Asia. Instead of finding Asia, Verrazano found what is now North Carolina. On March 7, Verrazano landed near the Cape Fear River. There he encountered Native Americans of the Algonquian tribes and mapped the Outer Banks. After returning to France, Verrazano attempted to secure funding for future trips to that area of the New World. France, however, was at war, and Verrazano's requests were denied, postponing France's interests in Columbus's New World.

The Spanish

In the summer of 1526 six Spanish ships carrying about six hundred people, including women, children, and black slaves, sailed from Hispaniola to the Cape Fear River area. Led by Lucas Vázquez de Ayllón, they wanted to start a new Spanish colony, but found the tidewater region unsuitable for growing their crops. In order to find drier, more fertile farmland, the group traveled south

Giovanni da Verrazano was looking for a shortcut to Asia when he discovered North Carolina.

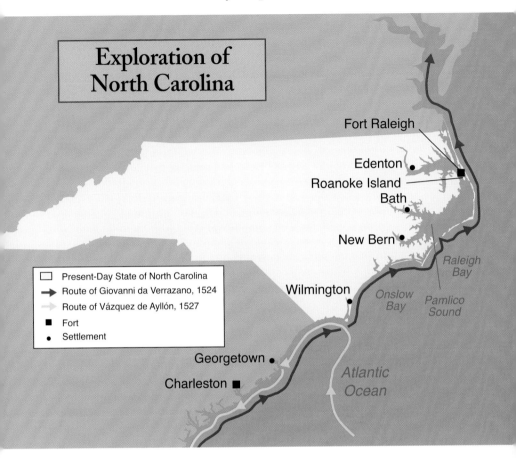

Exploration of North Carolina

Fort Raleigh

Edenton

Roanoke Island

Bath

New Bern

Raleigh Bay

Wilmington

Onslow Bay

Pamlico Sound

Georgetown

Atlantic Ocean

Charleston

Present-Day State of North Carolina

Route of Giovanni da Verrazano, 1524

Route of Vázquez de Ayllón, 1527

Fort

Settlement

toward what is now South Carolina. Many, including de Ayllón, fell ill or died from hunger or exhaustion. By October only 150 colonists remained. Discouraged, they built two small ships and returned to Hispaniola, ending Spain's hope of starting a new colony.

The English

Not wanting to be left out of the race for land in the New World, England's ruler, Queen Elizabeth I, gave Sir Walter Raleigh permission to send ships to the New World to find a good location for a colony.

Sir Walter Raleigh sailed to Roanoke Island with 108 men to establish a colony for England.

On July 13, 1584, two of Raleigh's best captains, Philip Amadas and Arthur Barlow, went ashore near what is now Kitty Hawk, North Carolina. The captains and their crew explored Bodie and Roanoke Islands and were impressed with the friendly Native Americans they encountered and the abundance of wild foods and cultivated crops growing in the area.

They decided that Roanoke would be able to support a colony, and even brought two Native Americans from the area—Wanchese and Manteo—with them when they reported their findings to Raleigh and the queen.

Over the next year, Raleigh assembled a team of 108 men to settle Roanoke. The team included a scientist named Thomas Hariot, an artist named John White, a military expert named Ralph Lane, and the Native Americans Manteo and Wanchese who would act as interpreters. On June 17, 1585, Raleigh's team, under the leadership of Sir Richard Grenville, landed at Croatan Island, fifty miles south of Roanoke. The English visited several villages on their way to Roanoke. On one such visit, a silver cup disappeared. Grenville and his men assumed that someone in the local village had taken the cup, and in retaliation they burned the entire village and its fields. This harsh treatment of local Native Americans would later play a key role in the fate of the colony.

Exploring New Lands

After reaching Roanoke in July, Grenville's team built a fort and spent the next year exploring their surroundings. John White documented what he saw and experienced in numerous drawings and descriptions. Ralph Lane and a few others struck out in search of gold and other precious metals. Thomas Hariot collected samples of native plants and small animals to take back to England. But, because of their earlier mistreatment of

John White sketched drawings like this one as he and Sir Richard Grenville's team explored Roanoke Island.

the Native Americans on Croatan Island, the English also encountered many conflicts with neighboring Native American tribes. To make matters worse, the Englishmen's food and material supplies were running out. Determined to see the colony succeed, Grenville returned to England for supplies early in 1586. By the spring, there was still no sign of Grenville and tensions between the English and the Native Americans had worsened. The settlers became discouraged.

On June 8 a small fleet of English ships command-ed by Sir Francis Drake landed on Roanoke Island. Drake and his men were returning to England after raiding Spanish ships in the Caribbean and Florida. They had orders from England to stop and inspect Sir Walter Raleigh's experimental colony. A hurricane struck the coast during Drake's visit. They gave up on Grenville and the colony and returned to England with Drake. England's first attempt at a colony in North Carolina had failed.

The Lost Colony

Despite his first failure, Sir Walter Raleigh sent anoth-er group of potential colonists to the land the English now called Virginia (after Queen Elizabeth I, who was called the "Virgin Queen" because she never married). The leader of this second group of 150 men, women, and children was John White, the artist who was a part of the original expedition. In July 1587 they landed at Roanoke Island and quickly started to rebuild the fort and cottages the first expedition had left behind.

A few days after their arrival, Native Americans from a nearby Roanoke tribe killed a colonist. In retal-iation, John White ordered an attack, but his men attacked the wrong tribe, killing and injuring innocent Croatoans. As a result, Native American tribes near the colonists refused to help them. The colonists had arrived too late in the year to plant crops, and without the help of local Native Americans, their survival was uncertain. At the end of the month John White sailed to England, hoping to return quickly with enough food and supplies to see the colonists through the winter. He did not return for three years.

When John White reached England, he found the country at war with Spain. This war, a shortage of funds, and severe storms kept White from Roanoke. When he finally returned in 1587, there was no trace of the colonists. One word—CROATOAN—had been carved into a tree in the settlement. When White

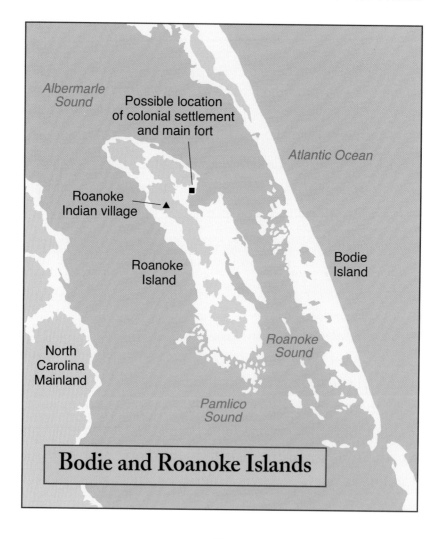

Albermarle
Sound

Possible location
of colonial settlement
and main fort

Atlantic Ocean

Roanoke
Indian village

Bodie
Island

Roanoke
Island

Roanoke
Sound

North
Carolina
Mainland

Pamlico
Sound

Bodie and Roanoke Islands

Looking for traces of the lost Roanoke colony, John White and his men found only the word CROATOAN *carved into a tree.*

and his crew set out for Croatan Island in search of the colonists, fierce storms forced them out to sea and back to England. White never returned to Roanoke, and no one ever found the colonists of England's Lost Colony. Once again, England had failed in its attempt to settle what is now North Carolina.

Chapter Three

The Settlers

In 1607 England established a colony at Jamestown near what is now Chesapeake, Virginia. Named for King James I, Jamestown quickly became a hub of activity, and by the 1650s was overcrowded. In 1653 Nathaniel Batts became the first to live south of Virginia when he built his two-room cabin in what is now Bertie County, North Carolina. Soon, hundreds of people were leaving Virginia for the area called Carolana.

Virginia colonists came to Carolana searching for good soil for growing tobacco, for freedom from Virginia's government, and even for gold. They built small, dirt floor log cabins and planted fields of corn, peas, potatoes, wheat, and sweet potatoes nearby. The settlers also fished, raised goats and chickens, and kept hogs, letting the hogs roam free in the woods and then slaughtering them for ham and bacon. Deer provided additional meat for the settlers, and deerskins were

Carolana settlers return home after a day of hunting game for meat, clothing, and bedding.

used for clothing and bedding. Any extra corn the farmers raised was traded in Virginia for items such as fabric, farming tools, guns, and gunpowder. Wild animal skins were also traded in Virginia, as was tobacco.

Life in the new territory was harsh, but by the 1660s almost five hundred people lived in Carolana. Runaway slaves, servants, poor farmers, and religious groups such as Quakers and Baptists made their homes there. In fact, the land became known as Rogues' Haven because so many of its settlers went there to escape persecution from English and colonial societies. As the new settlement, now called Carolina, continued to grow, Europeans, including the French,

A native Tuscarora visits new settlers in Rogues' Haven. Cheated and mistreated by the newcomers, the Tuscaroras fought back by raiding settlements.

German, and Swiss, joined the English colonists in Carolina to make new lives for themselves.

In 1706 the first permanent town was built in Carolina. Settled by a French religious group called the Huguenots, the town was named Bath in honor of one of the lords proprietors, John Granville, the Earl of Bath. Another city was built in 1710 near the place where the Neuse and Trent rivers meet. The Swiss and German settlers who founded the city named it New Bern in honor of the city of Bern in Switzerland. During the 1700s immigrants from Scotland settled places such as Scotland Neck and Scotland County. Other immigrants from Ireland and Germany left their home countries for the religious and political freedom found in Carolina. The slow but steady increase in population was good for the new territory, but it was not good for the Native Americans who lived there.

The Tuscarora War

The Tuscaroras were the largest tribe of Native Americans in northern Carolina and were severely mistreated by the white settlers. New settlers forced them off their tribal lands, stole their crops, and cheated them in trade deals. With more and more settlers moving into Carolina and pushing them further away from their land, the Tuscaroras decided to fight back.

On September 22, 1711, the Tuscaroras attacked settlements along the Pamlico and Neuse rivers. By the day's end, almost 130 settlers were killed. The Tuscaroras continued to raid settlements in northern Carolina until early in 1712, when Governor Edward Hyde asked southern Carolina for help. Colonel John Barnwell and five hundred men from southern Carolina came to Governor Hyde's aid and put an end to the Tuscarora raids, forcing the tribe to make a peace agreement and stop the raids. But, when colonists captured several Tuscaroras in the fall of that same year, the Tuscaroras felt betrayed and the raids started again. This time, southern Carolina sent Colonel James Moore, and he and his men defeated the Tuscaroras in a terribly bloody battle in March 1713 near what is now Snow Hill, North Carolina. All the Tuscarora forts were destroyed and almost one thousand Tuscarora were killed. The Tuscaroras surrendered, and by 1715 most of them had left Carolina to join their kinsmen, the Iroquois, in what is now New York.

Pirates

While Carolina was dealing with Tuscarora raids inland, it was also plagued by pirate raids on the coast. Pirates used northern Carolina's Outer Banks as a hideout and ambushed ships entering and leaving the colony. They captured these ships and stole whatever supplies they were carrying, sometimes killing the ships' crews. The pirates would then sell the supplies for high prices or keep the cargo—especially if it was gold, silver, or other valuables—for themselves.

The most famous of the Carolina pirates were Edward Teach, better known as Blackbeard, and Stede Bonnet, who was called the "Gentleman Pirate." In 1718

Lieutenant Robert Maynard (right) battles the pirate Blackbeard, famous for ambushing ships and stealing their cargo.

Colonel William Rhett captured Stede Bonnet after a fierce battle at sea. Bonnet was taken to the city of Charleston where he and about fifty other pirates were hanged. On November 22 of that same year, Lieutenant Robert Maynard encountered Blackbeard near Ocracoke

Island. During the fight, Blackbeard was shot and later beheaded. By the end of 1718 most pirates along the Carolina coast had been killed or imprisoned, marking the end of piracy on the Carolina coast.

Because pirates were no longer a serious threat along the Outer Banks, North Carolina was able to increase its shipments of tar, pitch, and turpentine to England. These items, called "naval stores," were used to build and repair ships, and because England could get these materials cheaper from Carolina than from

Settlers and escaped slaves work at a turpentine distillery. Turpentine and other "naval stores" were sold to England and used to repair ships.

Once piracy along the North Carolina coast was stopped, travel and trade became safe. As a result, European settlers became more interested in North Carolina.

countries in Europe, these materials were in high demand. More tar, pitch, and turpentine distilleries were built, which meant more jobs for settlers. This industry also earned northern Carolina settlers their nickname—Tar Heels—because tar is hard to remove from skin and clothing.

A Royal Colony

Despite conflicts with Native Americans and pirate raids on the coast, Carolina slowly but steadily grew in size. In 1712 the lords proprietors split the colony in two, forming North Carolina and South Carolina. The following year North Carolina's third town, Beaufort, was established, which was followed by Edenton in 1714. In 1729 another big change occurred in North Carolina when the lords proprietors sold their land rights to King George II of England. The sale of these property rights to the king made North Carolina a royal colony. This meant that the king would have the right to tax and govern the colony and provide it with military support and government funding. As a result, more European settlers became interested in North Carolina. Irish and German settlers moved into the western portion of North Carolina and created large, prosperous farming communities and formal schools and colleges. By the 1770s almost 300,000 people lived in North Carolina.

Chapter Four

The Twelfth State

As North Carolina grew in size, its citizens in the west felt they were not being fully represented in the colony legislature, which was filled with lawmakers primarily from the east. The western colonists organized a political group called the Regulators and printed and distributed flyers and pamphlets calling for government **reform** and an end to unfair taxes. But, when nothing was done to help their cause, the Regulators marched to the court in Hillsborough in December 1770. They ran the officials out and took over the court. The following spring, North Carolina's governor at the time, William Tryon, led a group of **militiamen** to Alamance County, just west of Hillsborough, to regain control of the courts and arrest the Regulators. When the Regulators refused to surrender, Governor Tryon ordered the militiamen to fire on their fellow North Carolinians. About a dozen men on both sides were killed and six Regulators were

Governor William Tryon orders his militiamen to fire on the Regulators.

captured and hanged for treason. Although this ended the internal conflict between eastern and western colonists in North Carolina, this was not the end of the struggle against unfair taxation.

From 1689 to 1763 England fought many wars against France and Spain for control of land in the New World. In the end, England found itself in control of vast amounts of land, but in a great deal of debt as well. In order to raise money, England began taxing its colonies. One tax required that all printed documents in the colonies carry an official stamp of the English government. Newspapers, wills, sale agreements, and other legal documents could not be printed or issued without the stamp. Another tax called the Townshend Duties was placed on items such as paper, glass, sugar, and tea. Outraged, colonists in all thirteen colonies began to form groups called the Sons of Liberty to protest the taxes, and in 1770 North Carolina refused to **import** products made in England.

The Sons of Liberty organized meetings like this one to protest English taxation of the colonies.

Changes in Government

North Carolina went a step further in its protest and formed its own government in 1774. Called the North Carolina Provincial Congress, it met in New Bern and elected three men, Richard Caswell, Joseph Hewes, and William Hopper, to represent the colony at the First Continental Congress. At the First Continental Congress, representatives from the colonies drafted a petition declaring that the taxes England forced on them were illegal because the colonists had no representation in the English **Parliament**. The petition asked the British government to end the taxation, but Britain would not back down, and in 1775 British troops and Patriots, as the colonists were called, fought in Lexington, Massachusetts. The Revolutionary War had begun.

While the Continental Congress worked out details for the war against Britain, North Carolina's Provincial Congress worked to set up a new government for the colony. In August 1775 the Provincial Congress organized district and county committees to govern the colony. The former governor, Josiah Martin, tried to organize a takeover in February 1776 with the help of British troops, but they were defeated at the Battle of Moore's Creek Bridge. Two months later on April 12, at the next Provincial Congress meeting, representatives voted to make North Carolina a free state. It became the first colony to declare its independence from England. When the Continental Congress voted on July 2, 1776, North Carolina representatives

Patriots battle British troops in North Carolina during the Revolutionary War.

and delegates from the other colonies voted for freedom from England, and on July 4, 1776, the Declaration of Independence was approved. Later that year, North Carolina's Provincial Congress created the state's first constitution and Richard Caswell was chosen as its first governor.

The war with Britain ended when a peace treaty was signed in 1783, but the peace treaty did not solve the many problems of the colonies. In fact, after the war there were even more problems than before. The states, as they were now called, were existing under laws called the Articles of Confederation. These laws gave each state its own power and hardly any to a central government. There was no president, no central court system, no capital, no national **currency**, and no taxes. Without these things, each state had its own system of government, its own money, and no way of knowing what the other states were doing. In order to

Benjamin Franklin addresses the members of the Constitutional Convention. North Carolina refused to accept the Constitution until the Bill of Rights was added.

make the states stronger, leaders from each state decided to meet in Philadelphia to construct a more organized government.

The Constitutional Convention, as the meeting was called, was held between May and September in 1787. Delegates to the convention came up with a new set of laws for all the states. Called the United States Constitution, the new laws created a central government with a president as its leader. The Constitution created a court system to rule in the states and over the states. It created a strong military, a Congress that was made up of representatives from each state, and a standard form of money for use within and between the states. Although this new form of government greatly improved conditions for the states, North Carolina's delegates refused to accept them. When the time came to vote, North Carolina's delegates did not **ratify** the Constitution.

The Twelfth State

North Carolina had been called Rogues' Haven because many of its early settlers had come to the state looking for political or religious freedom. The Constitution gave a great deal of power to the government, but it did not protect the freedoms of individuals. For this reason North Carolina, along with Rhode Island, refused to accept the new form of government. Leaders of the Constitutional Convention agreed that a Bill of Rights should be added to the Constitution. The Bill of Rights would guarantee individuals certain rights and protections from the government. In 1789, after work on the Bill of Rights was underway, North Carolina voted to accept the Constitution and became the twelfth state under the new U.S. Constitution. Known for their outspokenness and love of freedom, North Carolinians paved the way for all Americans to enjoy the freedoms granted by the Bill of Rights.

Facts About North Carolina

Largest city: Charlotte

State beverage: milk

State capital: Raleigh

State colors: red and blue

State song: "The Old North State" by William Gaston

State mammal: eastern gray squirrel

State motto: Essequam videri (To be, rather than to seem)

State bird: cardinal

State dog: plott hound

State fish: channel bass

State flower: dogwood

State insect: honey bee

State nickname: Tar Heel State

State rock: granite

State stone: emerald

State tree: Pine

State vegetable: sweet potato

Farm products: dairy, eggs, hogs, chickens, turkeys, cows, fish, soybeans, tobacco, apples, corn

Industries: telecommunications, furniture, paper products, medical, technology, textiles, tourism, seafood, tobacco products

Population: 2001: 8,186,268

70.2% White

21.6% African American

4.7% Latino/Hispanic

1.4% Asian

1.2% Native American

Famous people: David Brinkley, journalist; Curtis Brown, astronaut; John Coltrane, jazz musician; Clyde Edgerton, writer; Roberta Flack, singer/songwriter; Ava Gardner, actress; Billy Graham, minister; Andy Griffith, actor; Mia Hamm, athlete; Marion Jones, athlete; Michael Jordan, athlete; Charles Kuralt, journalist; Sugar Ray Leonard, athlete; Thelonius Monk, jazz musician; Richard Petty, NASCAR driver; Bob Timberlake, artist

Glossary

currency: Any form of money.

dialect: A language considered as part of a larger family of languages.

import: To bring goods from one country into another.

militiamen: Men who make up an army of citizens.

Parliament: The ruling body of England.

piedmont: Fertile region between the foothills of the Appalachian Mountains and the Atlantic coast.

ratify: To approve.

reform: Improvements made by removing errors or faults.

tidewater: Low-lying coastal lands drained by streams.

For Further Exploration

Books

Hugh Talmage Lefler, *North Carolina, The History of a Southern State.* Chapel Hill: University of North Carolina Press, 1963. Examines the history, geography, and ethnic makeup of the state.

Hugh Talmage Lefler and William Powell, *Colonial North Carolina; A History.* New York: Scribner, 1973. Describes the beginnings of the Tar Heel state.

Thomas C. Parramore, *Carolina Quest.* New Jersey: Prentice-Hall, 1978. Explores the search for identity and community from colonial times to the bicentennial.

William Powell, *The North Carolina Colony.* New York: Crowell-Collier, 1969. Follows North Carolina from its colonial beginnings to statehood.

Websites

State Library of North Carolina (http://statelibrary.dcr. state.nc.us). Website version of the North Carolina Encyclopedia.

North Carolina (www.visitnc.com). Tourism site for the state of North Carolina.

NC@ your service (www.ncgov.com). Official website for the state of North Carolina.

Index

North Carolina

Picture Credits

About the Author

A native of North Carolina, Teresa L. Hyman is a professional editor and writer living in Overland Park, Kansas. She is the mother of two children, Briana and Devin, and enjoys studying African American literature and art.

HICKMANS